NOT JUST WHAT YOU SEE THE SUPER POWER IN ME

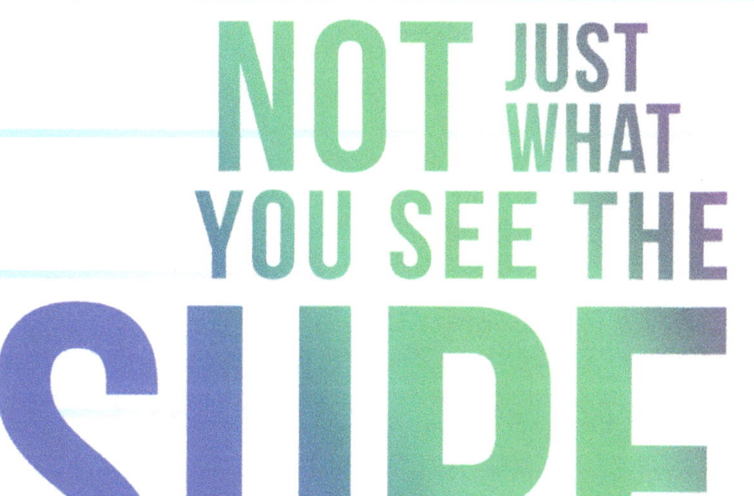

WRITTEN BY
Ryan Williams

ILLUSTRATED BY **Christina Brown**

Library of Congress Cataloging-in-Publication Data.

Printed in the United States of America.

Illustration by Christina Brown
Book Production by Nikiea

this book belongs to:

"Humanity starts within"

This book is dedicated to any
kid that's battling cancer or
everyday life challenges.
Don't loose Hope, Don't loose
Courage and Never Give Up!

I light up
the world

In the company of humans searching for a meaning,

I am a lion

I was designed to stand out in a crowd.

My superpower, Cancer
cured me that way.

I was only two at the time just perfected the art of walking.
Today I am here talking. Bless my ancestors
I am me for me.

Life is deeper than just living
I am here. Somehow my mind ventures within the
thoughts of deaths greatest victims.
We can't all afford to see the same. Think the same,
Be the same. Edit someone's life frame by frame.
My eyes are of the difference. I am physically and
mentally equally different looking for peace
and teach my existence
No harm no foul just love yourself love your health
Healing the past creates healthy soil for growing a
better future.
We sometimes bury the past without even touching
the surface.
That is to say... As a society the experiences of the
past are not fully understood until the future
recreates them.

More Love More Life More Peace Love Yourself.

Love
yourself

Clothes cover my body not my mind.

Provide style and speak to the world around me

Clothes come in all shapes and sizes.

Some wear clothes as disguises

Sort of like a superhero to hide his or her identity

Some clothes are uniforms and tell a story of a job.

Firefighters fight fires.

Nurses and Doctors fight disease and bacteria.

Police Officers sworn to protect and serve the community.

Soldiers from far away protect the home where we stay

Clothes are very special and show others my culture the strength of my ancestors

Clothes in a storm keep me warm, on a bright day a baseball cap keeps the sun away

Clothes are my superpower.

My clothes express and show how I feel

My face maybe different.

So, what I can still be a fashion model. We play like it's a dirt bike and

press the throttle. We keep going!!!

Skin and all Wheelchair and all hair may fall I wear what I love to bring peace and unity.

My difference causes no harm and together my clothes keep hearts forever warm

Forever beautiful

My skin is beautiful my skin is lovely my skin is me
My skin colors me like a painting of the world
Brown Blue Black yellow orange green and every
color in between together blend Kings and Queens
My skin is lovely and upright. If you look closely
you may find a treasure map that connects us
all together
My skin, old or young, always fresh, lines and all
stretches near and far
My skin is lovely and powerful enough to ignite a
candle to fade away darkness in the night
Freckles, moles, tiny dots, and little spots make
my skin equally unique
My skin forever beautiful
My skin is my super power

I am not
alone

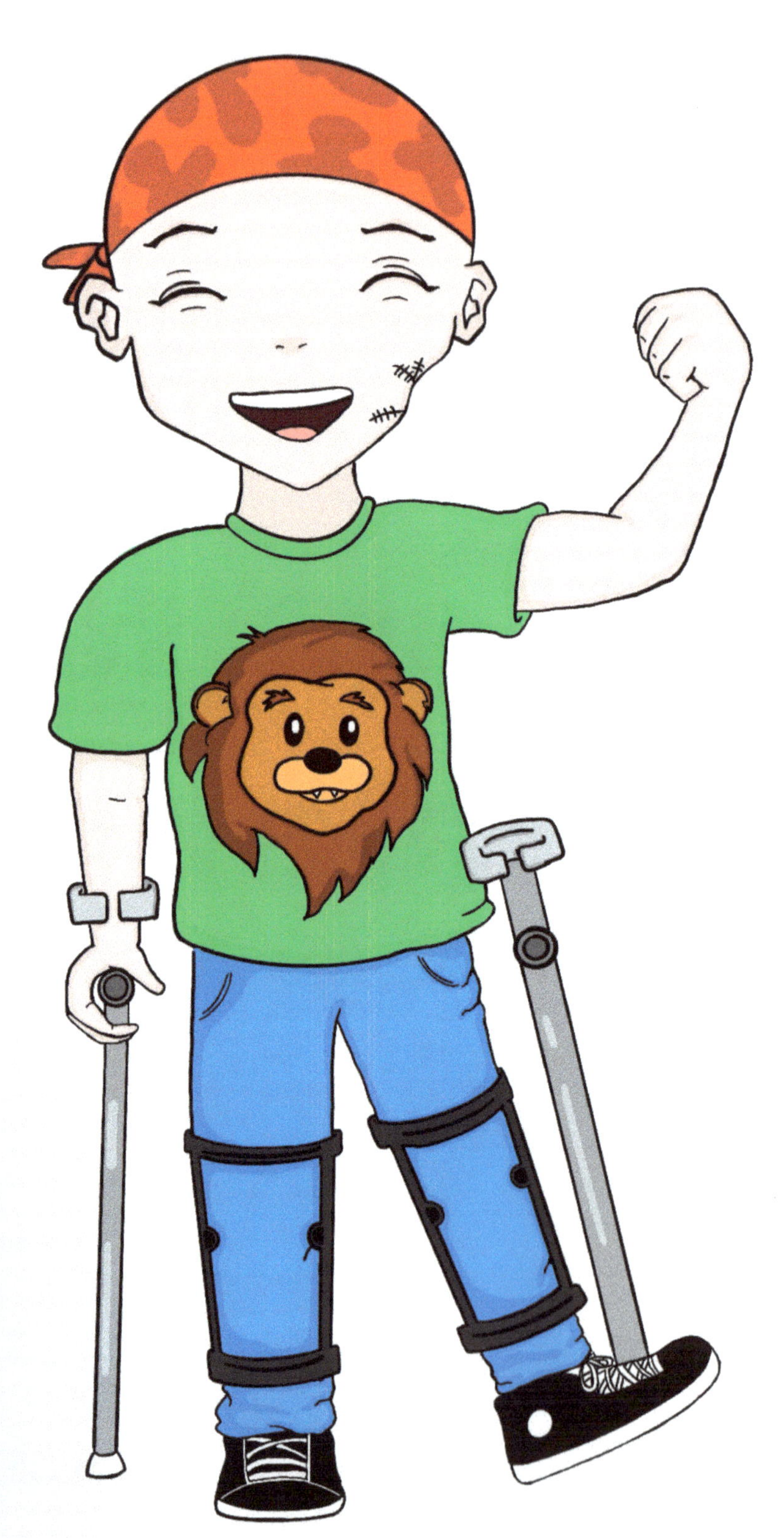

Red Green Yellow Blue what kind of
face are you
One two three four I am not only my
face I am much more

Ni hao, Hola, Bonjour,

Hi my name is

I am smart I am strong I am awesome
my face is not my only super power
I can read write draw and type
Five Six Seven Eight today will be
awesomely great
I can run fast and jump high almost
touching the sky
Brave, honest and happy to be me
showing the world how amazingly
awesome we can all be!!!

One of a kind

SUPER

Skinny, Heavy, Big or Small we are equal all in all.
One two three I love me
I'm not ugly, I'm uniquely different, one of a Kind
One two three I love me
I'm not too fat, I'm healthy and strong, more is
better!! I can dance run and jump high
One two three I love me
I'm not too skinny I can eat and lift an ocean
One two three I love me
We walk together we talk with love not hate, we
laugh for happiness and we create peace for fun
One two three love me

Differences are
what create
unity.

SUPER!

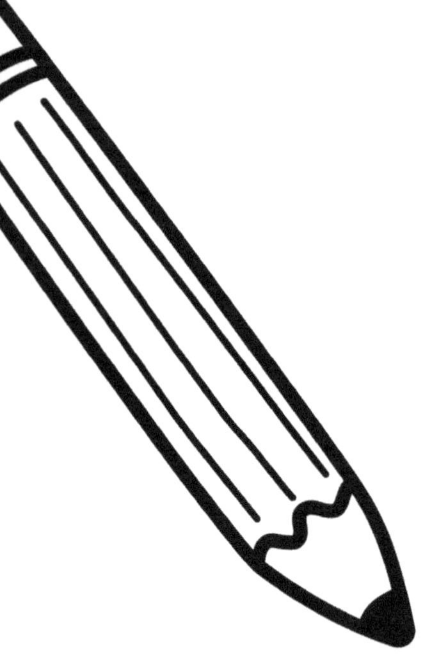

Free Space

About Reform Deformity

Reform Deformity is a heart centered organization that focuses on bringing awareness to individuals who have been psychically deformed due to injury, surgery and or illness. However deformities are not only found on the outside but also in the inside of ones being. No one is perfect or normal. One is to be educated to see with the mind and heart and not only with sight alone. That is to say the deformity awareness movement will educate the community through stories, events and fundraisers on how to break the barriers of associating an individuals looks with his or her intelligence, social status or behavior. People will be different but it is not up to us to determine where someone belongs but rather build a path of accurate communication and overall acceptance.

meet Ryan

About the Author

Ryan Williams

Author, Poet, Photographer, and Cancer Survivor

Differences are what creates unity. At the age of 2, my mom noticed there were no teeth growing on the side left side of my face. Diversity and individuality spark curiosity. At the age of 2 in 1991 I was diagnosed with a rare type of childhood cancer. From what I remember it started out as a regular doctor's appointment to me. My mom noticed there were no teeth growing on the left side of my mouth which sparked curiosity.

She was startled and took me to my pediatric doctor. Within seconds of examination, my doctor told my mother it was cancer. My mother then took me to Sinai hospital where I was diagnosed with Rhabdomyosarcoma. There was a small chance I would survive. I remember my family coming to visit me during chemotherapy and the other children that were receiving treatment as well. Through the Make a Wish foundation I was offered a trip to Disney World and I said yes!! I was then sent to Disney World with my family which was amazing. Through prayer, love, and unity among those who cared for me I am now 30 years cancer free. However, the radiation and chemotherapy left me with what medical professionals label as facial deformity. I feel it to be simply my difference. I use my difference and my story, to inspire and educate others.

I am the owner and operator of Reform Deformity. An organization that aims to reduce stigma and indifference among individuals with deformities through education and inspirational stories. We will inspire individuals to unbox their thoughts for old stigma and social norms to create new insight into equality.

Reform
Deformity

www.reformdeformity.org

www.ingramcontent.com/pod-product-compliance
Lightning Source LLC
Chambersburg PA
CBHW041819110726
48006CB00019B/2441